THE
RUSSIAN
EXPEDITIONARY
FORCE
IN FRANCE 1916-1918

FREDERICK ASHMORE

AuthorHouse™ UK
1663 Liberty Drive
Bloomington, IN 47403 USA
www.authorhouse.co.uk
UK TFN: 0800 0148641 (Toll Free inside the UK)
UK Local: 02036 956322 (+44 20 3695 6322 from outside the UK)

Because of the dynamic nature of the Internet, any web addresses or links contained in this book may have changed since publication and may no longer be valid. The views expressed in this work are solely those of the author and do not necessarily reflect the views of the publisher, and the publisher hereby disclaims any responsibility for them.

Any people depicted in stock imagery provided by Getty Images are models, and such images are being used for illustrative purposes only.
Certain stock imagery © Getty Images.

This book is printed on acid-free paper.

ISBN: 978-1-6655-9836-1 (sc)
ISBN: 978-1-6655-9835-4 (e)

Print information available on the last page.

Published by AuthorHouse 05/20/2022

authorHOUSE

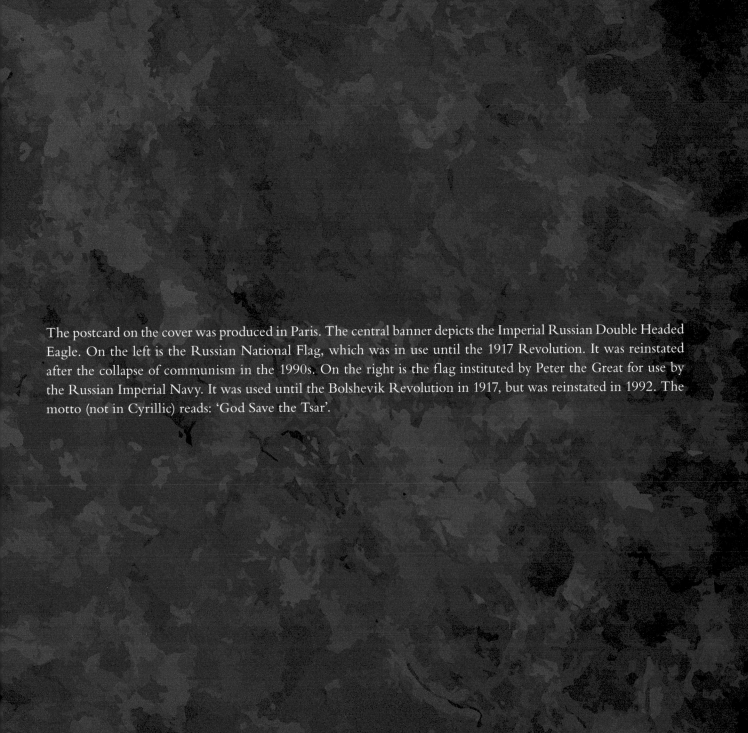

The postcard on the cover was produced in Paris. The central banner depicts the Imperial Russian Double Headed Eagle. On the left is the Russian National Flag, which was in use until the 1917 Revolution. It was reinstated after the collapse of communism in the 1990s. On the right is the flag instituted by Peter the Great for use by the Russian Imperial Navy. It was used until the Bolshevik Revolution in 1917, but was reinstated in 1992. The motto (not in Cyrillic) reads: 'God Save the Tsar'.

CONTENTS

INTRODUCTION

This book of postcards and photographs is not a history, but a pictorial record of the service in France of the Russian Expeditionary Force 1916-1918. Four brigades were selected to serve in the French Army. They were the 1st, 2nd, 3rd and 4th Brigades. The 1st and 3rd Brigades were to remain in France, and the 2nd and 4th were to join the French Army in Salonika.

This is a brief account of events leading up to their arrival and a summary of subsequent events. A political agreement eventually resulted in the transfer of four brigades to the French Army in 1916. A decision was made to avoid the U-boat infested North Sea. The first troops would travel via the Trans-Siberian Railway to Manchuria, and then again by rail to arrive, via Manchuria, at Darien (it was renamed in 1981 and became Dalian) on the Yellow Sea. At Darien three ships, the *Admiral Latouche Treville*, *Himalaya* and *Sontay*, which the French had impounded at Saigon, would then proceed on the long voyage to Marseille.

These photographs show the *Latouche Treville* at Darien with the Russian troops waiting to board.

And a scene on board, which was taken in Japanese waters and gives the idea of the gross overcrowding. The voyage must have been extremely uncomfortable for the rank and file.

The troops departed Moscow in early February 1916 and arrived at Marseille in April. The 3rd Brigade was more fortunate and departed Archangel by sea for Brest, then by rail to Marseille, and then to Mirabeau Camp.

They were received by a French delegation at the port followed by a triumphal march through the streets of the city and a tumultuous welcome by the citizens of Marseille. The crowd saw the troops arrival as their salvation because the French Army had suffered heavy casualties.

After a few days at Mirabeau Camp near Marseille the brigade entrained for Mailly-le-Camp (a large military training camp built in 1902) located in the Champagne-Ardenne. They were issued with French rifles, the Lebel, and eventually with the Adrian steel helmet albeit with the Russian military badge. They were not impressed with either the steel helmets nor the gas masks. After their training the 1st Brigade joined the French Army in the Suippes–Fort Pompelle area near Reims. The Russians fought well to the point of recklessness. But in 1917, the year of revolution in Russia, troops began to hold political meetings and discipline collapsed. The French relocated the two brigades to La Courtine, an old French training area near the town of Millevaches, and left the problem to the Russians to sort out. The outcome was the end of the Russian Expeditionary Force. Many men returned to Russia, but some remained loyal to the French, and these were eventually formed into the Russian Legion. Initially, the legion was allocated to a Moroccan Division. After the armistice they were located at Worms in Germany, from where they were returned to Mailly to be disbanded.

Frederick Ashmore

Note: for details of the Russian Expeditionary Force in France I would recommend the book by J.H. Cockfield With Snow on Their Boots *published in 1998, Macmillan Press Ltd.*

ARRIVAL IN MARSEILLE

LES TROUPES RUSSES A MARSEILLE
20 Avril 1916
Sur l'avant du Latouche-Tréville

At last - Marseille.

The arrival at Marseille of the *Latouche Treville* on 20 April 1916. The ship was named after a French Vice Admiral, Louis René Madeleine Levassor, comte de Latouche-Tréville (1745-1804) who fought in the American War of Independence.

NOS ALLIÉS A MARSEILLE — Au môle D, le Général Menissier monte à bord du « Latouche-Treville ».

OUR ALLIES IN MARSEILLES — At Mole D. General Menissier going ou board the « Latouche-Treville »

Visé, Paris (E.D)

The official welcome party, headed by General Ménissier (Alphonse Charles Louis Ménissier born Wissembourg, Bas-Rhin, Alsace, France) the Military Governor of Marseille, wait while the ship completes its docking procedure.

LES TROUPES RUSSES A MARSEILLE
20 Avril 1916
Salut à l'hymne Russe et à la Marseillaise

Photo Florca

The welcome party saluting while the national anthems of Russia and France are played.

2 — LES TROUPES RUSSES A MARSEILLE
Présentation de l'Etat-major Russe — L R.

This postcard appears to depict officers assembling prior to the official introductions.

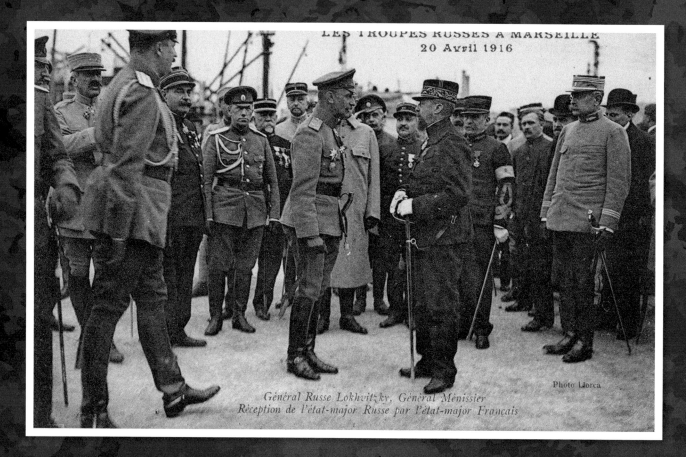

LES TROUPES RUSSES A MARSEILLE
20 Avril 1916

Général Russe Lokhvitzky, Général Ménissier
Réception de l'état-major Russe par l'état-major Francais

Photo Llorca

This group of officers are being presented to General Ménissier.

Major General Lokhvitsky, the commander of the 1ˢᵗ Brigade, in conversation with General Ménissier. Major General Nikolai Alexandrovich Lokhvitsky, the Order of St George, Fourth Class.

LES TROUPES RUSSES A MARSEILLE
20 Avril 1916

Photo Llorca

Two British officers in conversation with a nurse. General Ménissier is possibly on the left of the picture. Russian troops who have just disembarked can be seen in the background.

The band leading the troops forming up for the march past on the quayside.

4 - LES TROUPES RUSSES A MARSEILLE - La Musique — *L R.*

The march past is underway. This card has been annotated by the French as 'La Musique'.

5 - LES TROUPES RUSSES A MARSEILLE - Le Défilé Russe - L R

The Russian troops marching behind the band; their drill looks good. They are carrying Russian rifles shortly to be exchanged for the French 'Lebel'.

10 — LES TROUPES RUSSES A MARSEILLE
Les prisonniers Allemands regardant le Défilé Russe — *L R.*

German prisoners of war watching the march past of the newly arrived Russians of the 1st Brigade. The French guard is from Infantry Regiment 145. The French officer on his right seems to be bemused by the situation.

1 — L'ARMÉE RUSSE A MARSEILLE - Le Débarquement

The 3rd Brigade?

Although this postcard is annotated 'Le Débarquement' [leaving the ship] at Marseille, the troops appear to be embarking. The photograph bears no resemblance to the scenes of the arrival of the 1st Brigade. It is possible that this card depicts the loading of the 2nd Brigade commanded by General Mikhail Diterikhs, which had departed from Archangel on 4 July 1916 and had arrived at Brest (France) by sea on 18 July, and then travelled by rail to Marseille arriving on 21 July. Three days later they embarked for the remainder of their journey to Salonika by sea to become part of l'Armée de l'Orient commanded by General Sarrail.

MARCH PAST IN MARSEILLE

NOS ALLIÉS A MARSEILLE — Défilé des Troupes Russes. Général Lohvitski en tête, devant la Préfecture.

OUR ALLIES IN MARSEILLES — Russian troops defiling, General Lohvitski a head of them before the Prefecture.

Visé, Paris

The Russian Brigade paraded through the streets of Marseille to an enthusiastic welcome from the citizens of the city. The brigade commander Major General Lokhvitsky on the left of this picture can be seen saluting.

NOS ALLIES A MARSEILLE — Officiers Russes et Anglais, en compagnie du Général Menissier, assistent au Défilé.

OUR ALLIES IN MARSEILLES — Russian and English Officers in company with General Menissier look at the defiling troops

Visé, Paris

Taking the salute.

This postcard has been annotated in French and English 'OUR ALLIES IN MARSEILLE'. Russian and English officers in company with General Ménissier take the salute.

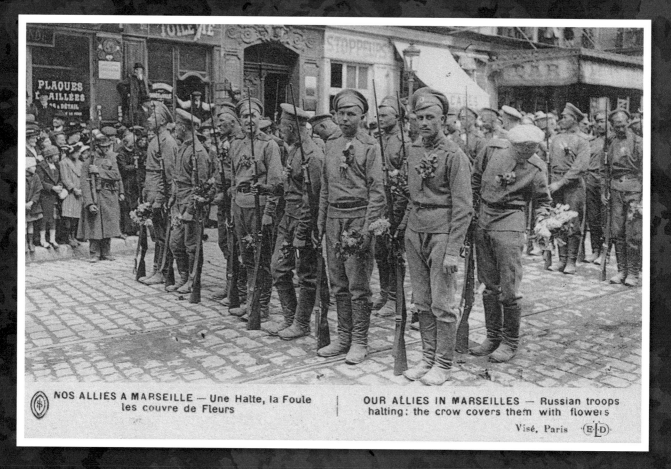

NOS ALLIES A MARSEILLE — Une Halte, la Foule les couvre de Fleurs

OUR ALLIES IN MARSEILLES — Russian troops halting: the crow covers them with flowers

Visé, Paris

'Stand Easy'.

The troops take a breather from the march past in Marseille. The flowers were distributed by the citizens of Marseille, many of whom can be seen in this postcard on the crowded pavement.

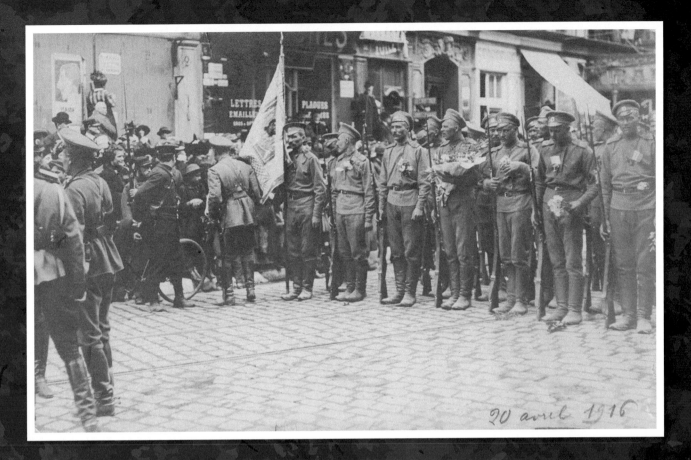

The flag of Imperial Russia.

A view taken from the same position. In this case, the flag bearer can be seen carrying the flag of Imperial Russia. There seems to be some problem with a bicycle!

MIRABEAU CAMP

Photo-Llorca

LES TROUPES RUSSES A MARSEILLE - Au Camp de Mirabeau
Visite du Camp par le Général Menissier, les officiers Russes, M. Dalimier sous-secrétaire d'état au Beaux-Arts

A tour of Mirabeau Camp.

This postcard is titled 'A Visit to the Camp by General Ménissier and M. Dalimier, Under Secretary of State for the Beaux-Arts'.

LES TROUPES RUSSES A MARSEILLE
Au Camp de Mirabeau, groupe d'officiers Alliés fraternisant

Edit T. Chabanian et Prebois. 12, rue Grignan

17/6 1916

Camp Mirabeau appears to have been a tented camp and was probably a transit camp. It was close to Marseille which was used by troopships bound to and from the east; Italy, Salonika, Egypt, Suez, and India were all military destinations. This postcard shows a mixed group of men probably in transit. The group consists of Russians, a British officer, two men from a Scottish regiment, an unidentified soldier between them, and one on the right.

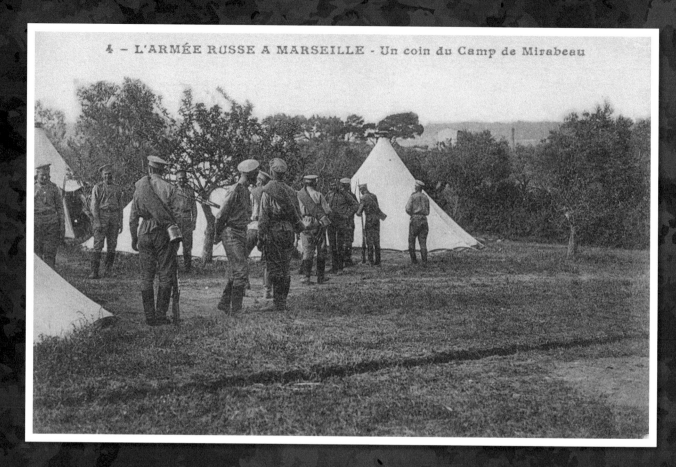

4 – L'ARMÉE RUSSE A MARSEILLE - Un coin du Camp de Mirabeau

Russian troops at Camp Mirabeau. They appear to be disorganised, and it is possible that they had just arrived from Marseille. The card is dated 7 June 1916.

LES TROUPES RUSSES A MARSEILLE
Au Camp de Mirabeau
La Revue des Troupes Russes par le Général Ménissier, Gouverneur de Marseille

General Ménissier reviewing Russian troops at Camp Mirabeau.

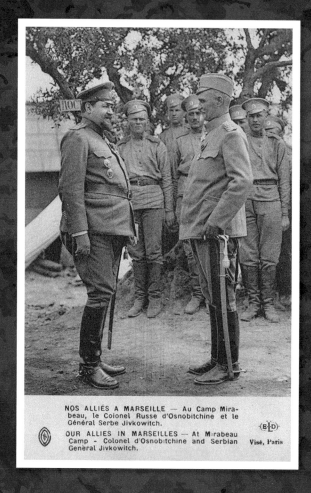

NOS ALLIÉS A MARSEILLE — Au Camp Mira-beau, le Colonel Russe d'Osnobitchine et le Général Serbe Jivkowitch.

OUR ALLIES IN MARSEILLES — At Mirabeau Camp - Colonel d'Osnobitchine and Serbian General Jivkowitch.

Visé, Paris

This meeting took place at Mirabeau Camp. An interesting postcard, but unfortunately I am unable to write much about it. Colonel d'Ostnobitchine can be seen on postcards associated with the 1st Brigade. It is possible that he was on the Headquarters Staff of the brigade.

The Serbian General Jivkowitch is also an unknown quantity, and I have not been able to find any details of his career.

Austria/Hungary declared war on Serbia on 28 July 1914. They were defeated by Serbia. However on 6 October 1915 the Serbian army was defeated by an army commanded by General von Mackensen enabling the central powers to occupy Serbia.

NOS ALLIÉS A MARSEILLE — Au Camp Mirabeau - Installation des Lavabos.

OUR ALLIES IN MARSEILLES — At Mirabeau
Camp - Lavatories installation.

Visé, Paris

An informal photograph of the 'wash place' at Camp Mirabeau.

5 – L'ARMÉE RUSSE A MARSEILLE – Le Lavabo au Camp de Mirabeau

This group is well aware of the camera. Some men appear relaxed others are 'standing to attention'.

NOS ALLIÉS A MARSEILLE — Nos Alliés au Repos. | OUR ALLIES IN MARSEILLES — Our Allies at rest. Visé, Paris

Off-duty soldiers relaxing at Camp Mirabeau.

7 – L'ARMÉE RUSSE A MARSEILLE - Parade à l'entrée du Camp de Mirabeau

A parade at Camp Mirabeau, probably prior to an exercise.

THE ORDER OF ST GEORGE

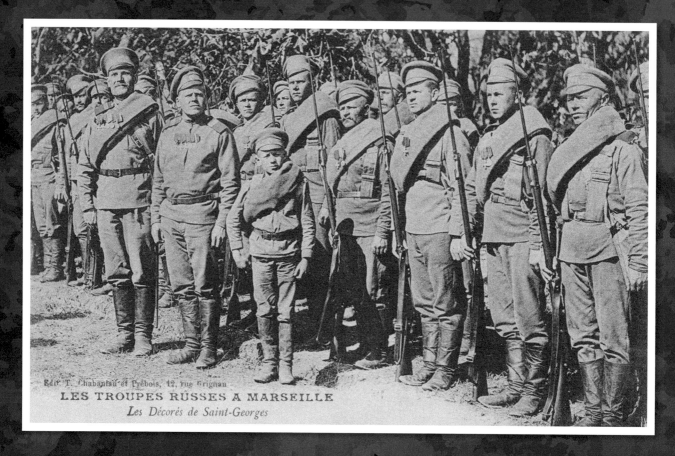

LES TROUPES RUSSES A MARSEILLE
Les Décorés de Saint-Georges

At least five soldiers in this group are wearing the medal the Cross of St George.

The Order of St George was established on 26 November 1769 by the Empress Catherine. There were several classes of this medal. Classes one to four were awarded to officers and five and six to NCOs.

BOY SOLDIERS

Edit. T. Chabanian et Prébois, 12, rue Grignan
LES TROUPES RUSSES A MARSEILLE
Kostia 11 ans et Vassile 12 ans
Engagés volontaires

Several boy soldiers have appeared on postcards. The first postcard is of Kostia, aged eleven years, and Vassile, aged twelve years. Kostia is very self-assured and is determined to steal the limelight.

Le plus jeune Combattant Russe
âgé de 12 ans

This postcard is dated in manuscript on the reverse 'Mailly 22 August 1916'. The boy is not named but his age is given as twelve years. (More about Mailly later.)

LES TROUPES RUSSES A MARSEILLE - La Musique

A more formidable band than that which we saw on the quayside at Marseille. The boy in the centre front row could possibly be Kostia.

MAILLY-LE-CAMP

Souvenir de Mailly-le-Camp

Bazar Militaire, A. Nieps

Mailly-le-Camp is situated in the department of the Aube. It was built in 1902 and was the largest training camp in France. The 1st Brigade arrived at the camp in the summer of 1916, the 3rd Brigade arrived in September of the same year.

ՅԱՂԹԱՆԱԿ ԹՈՒՐԻՆԿԱՆԱ

Guerre 1914-15-16... Les Russes au Camp de Mailly - Le Drapeau | War 1914-15-16... The Russians at Mailly Camp - The Flag

Visé, Paris No 1991

66me Série

A display of the Imperial Standard of Tsar Nicolas II. The 1st Brigade commander, Major General Lokhvitsky is standing second from the right.

Poincaré

CAMP DE MAILLY — Le Président passe sur le front des Troupes

Лагерь Майльи. — Президентъ Французской Республики проходитъ по фронту Русскихъ Войскъ.

Reproduction interdite
Visé, Paris No 767

A visit to Mailly-le-Camp by President Poincaré. The visit took place on 26 May 1916. He inspected the troops and presented medals to Major General Lokhvitsky.

The reverse of this postcard is also of interest. The card is dated in manuscript 22 August 1917. It is written in French and is addressed to the sender's godmother in Paris:

> My Dear godmother,
>
> I received your letter and your small parcel which gives me great pleasure. I thank you very much.
>
> As always I am well, will have rest at La Courtine Camp. The weather is good. Awaiting your good news, I send

Президентъ Пуанкаре награждаетъ генерала Лохвицкаго орденомъ Почетнаго Легіона.

Le President de la République décore le Général Lochvitzky de la croix de commandeur de la Légion d'Honneur.

Major General Lokhvitsky receiving the Légion d'Honneur from the President of France, Poincaré.

The Légion d'Honneur is the highest French Order of Merit for military and civil excellence.

MAILLY-le-CAMP. - La Chapelle Russe

The Russian Church at Mailly Camp.

When President Poincaré visited the camp on 26 May 1916 he visited the Russian church. After viewing the icons the priest gave a short speech in which he thanked the French for building the church.

CAMP de MAILLY. - Troupes Russes sortant de l'Office

A. Verry, éditeur

Russian officers leaving the church.

MAILLY-LE CAMP — Défilé des Troupes russes - La Musique

Русскія Войска. — Оркестръ.

Reproduction interdite

Visé, Paris
N° 407

A parade passing through the town of Mailly.

MAILLY-LE-CAMP — Défilé des Troupes russes - Le Drapeau

Русскія Войска. — Знамя.

Visé, Paris N° 407

Another parade through the town, possibly the same occasion. The Imperial Standard is being displayed.

MAILLY-LE-CAMP — Défilé des Troupes russes
Les Cuisines roulantes

Русскія Войска; Походныя Кухни.

Visé, Paris
Nº 407

Mobile kitchens passing through the town of Mailly.

MAILLY-LE-CAMP — Défilé des Troupes russes - Mitrailleurs

Русскія Войска. — Пулеметчики.

The caption on this postcard mentions 'machine guns', but these do not appear to be visible.

A good group photograph of Russian soldiers at Mailly-le-Camp. It is a posed group picture, possibly the men being specially selected. The senior soldier is probably seated on the left, he is the only one not carrying a rifle.

Troops with fixed bayonets, possibly leaving the camp for an exercise.

MAILLY-LE-CAMP — Enterrement d'un Officier russe

· Похороны русскаго офицера.

The funeral of a Russian officer at Mailly-le-Camp. The priest on the left is possibly Father Andrei Bogolovsky. He was very popular with rank and file, and was severely wounded in the closing days of the war. He died of his wounds shortly after the armistice.

MAILLY-LE-CAMP — Enterrement d'un Officier russe

Похороны русскаго офицера.

Reproduction interdite

Visé, Paris

Another funeral of a Russian officer. On this card three nurses can be seen following the bearers. On checking the 'Liste de personnel present a l'Ambulance de la 1ˢᵗ Brigade Spécial Russe' the names of three Russian nurses are listed – Mademoiselle Romanoff (sic), Madame Anoutchine and Madame Mokrzetsky. They are the only Russian nurses listed.

166   GRANDES MANŒUVRES.

Le Général Palitzine, Chef d'Etat-Major de l'armée russe et le Général de Lacroix, Directeur des Manœuvres. — *ND Phot.*

On the left is General Feodor Palitzin, and to the right the Director of Manoeuvres, a French general Henri de Lacroix. General Palitzin was responsible for all the Russian troops in France. This is possibly at Mailly-le-Camp.

BASTILLE DAY PARADE
PARIS
14 JULY 1916

L'ACTUALITÉ PAR LA CARTE POSTALE (1916). — UN 14 JUILLET HISTORIQUE
Nos Alliés Russes défilent sur les boulevards   Visé Paris 9..1.

The Imperial Standard paraded in Paris by the 1st Brigade. The marching drill appears to be impeccable.

" Le 14 Juillet à PARIS en 1916 " — Les Russes défilant Rue Royale

The Russians marching past.

Another view of the Russian contingent on the Bastille Day Parade. The crowds of spectators gave the Russians a good reception.

KING NICHOLAS

A visit to the troops of the 1ˢᵗ Brigade by King Nicholas I of Montenegro. Nicholas (1841–1921), assumed the title of king in 1910. Having previously served ten years as Sovereign Prince, he was gazetted Field Marshal of the Russian Army by the Tsar of Russia on the occasion of his jubilee. After the defeat of the Serbs by Austro-German forces he went into exile in France. While in exile he was accorded all the honours due to a Field Marshal. This photograph was taken at Châlons-sur-Marne.

King Nicholas I with Major General Lokhvitsky at Châlons–sur–Marne.

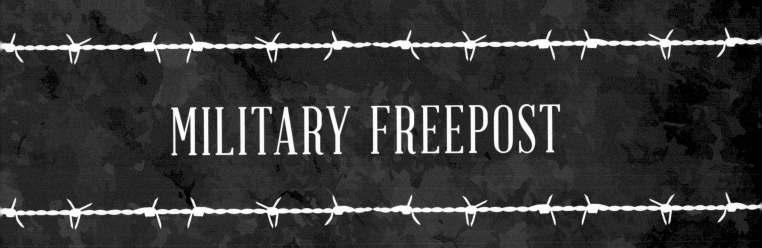

MILITARY FREEPOST

An unused postcard issued to Russian troops of the Russian Expeditionary Force in France 1916–1918. It is a simple postcard which requires details of the sender such as his name, regiment, etc. The flags are those of France and Russia.

MEMORIALS

This memorial commemorates 291 unidentified Russian soldiers of the 2nd Special Infantry Regiment of the 1st Special Brigade who are buried in a mass grave in this area. It is inscribed with the following words: *"Frenchmen, when the enemy is no longer in your fields and you can wander freely there, remember us and pick some flowers for us"*.

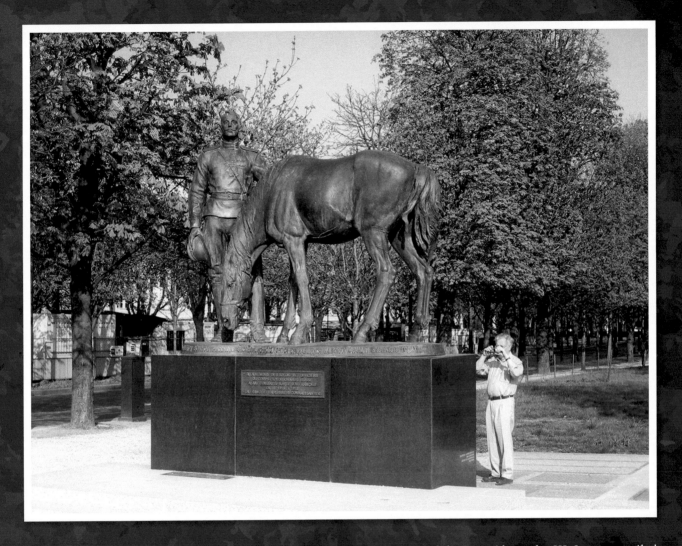

This memorial is situated on the Course du Reine near the River Seine and the Pont Alexandre III. It was unveiled on 21 June 2011 by the then Prime Minister of Russia, Vladimir Putin and Francois Fillon, Prime Minister of France.

ACKNOWLEDGEMENTS

Photographs
Memorial at Mourmelon–Vladimir Pomortzeff/Alamy Stock Photo
Monument in Paris–Anne Ashmore

Printed in the United States
by Baker & Taylor Publisher Services